OUTLINE OF THE HISTORY OF KALINGA

OUTLINE OF THE HISTORY OF KALINGA

R. C. MAJUMDAR

GYAN

Published by

Gyan Publishing House
5, Ansari Road
Daryaganj, New Delhi-110002
Phone: 011-47034999, 9811692060
E-mail: books@gyanbooks.com

Distribution Network
gyanbooks.com
India, USA, Canada, UK, Australia, France

ISBN : 978-81-212-3867-0 (PB)

2nd Impression 2020

Printed at: Gyan Press, Delhi.

Outline of the History of Kalinga
Author: R. C. Majumdar

OUTLINE OF THE HISTORY OF KALINGA.

Dr. R. C. Majumdar, M.A., Ph. D.

INTRODUCTION

I propose to discuss in this paper, very briefly, the main landmarks in the history of Kaliṅga for a period of more than seven hundred years, from the conquest of Samudragupta to the accession of Anantavarman Coḍaganga in 999 Śaka (1078 A. D.). Although the time is not yet ripe for writing a detailed history of the period, it would be useful, as a necessary preliminary to such study, to prepare a skeleton or framework of political history by a critical and comprehensive study of all the available data.

Much speculation has been made regarding the boundaries of Kaliṅga. There is no doubt that they varied from time to time. Without going into this vexed question I would assume, for the purpose of the present paper, that the country extended from the Mahānadī to the Godāvarī river.[1]

1. On the extent and boundaries of Kaliṅga, cf. the views of Dr. S. K. Aiyangar (J.A.H.R.S. Vol. II. pp. 1ff.) and Pandit Nilkantha Das (pp. 13 ff.)

The first definite idea of the political history of Kaliṅga, during the period under review, is obtained from the Allahabad Pillar inscription of Samudragupta. Among the kingdoms in the south, conquered by the great emperor, Piṣṭapura and Devarāṣṭra may be definitely placed in this region. The former name is even now represented by Pithapuram, while the kingdom of Devarāṣṭra must be located in the Vizagapatam district.

Several other kingdoms have been doubtfully located in this region. Kurāla has been taken as Kerala and identified with the Sonepur territory. Koṭṭura has been identified with Kothoor in the Ganjam district. Eraṇḍapalla is also believed to have been situated near Chicacole. None of these identifications rests, however, on a very secure basis, and in the opinion of some scholars, each of these is to be located south of the Godāvarī river.

For the period succeeding the Gupta conquest we get quite a large number of inscriptions giving us a long list of kings. These may be divided into the three following groups :—

I. Early Kaliṅga kings.
II. Early Gāṅga kings.
III. Later Gāṅga kings.

By this last we have to understand the kings of the Gāṅga dynasty mentioned in the copper-plates of Anantavarman Coḍa-Gaṅga and his grandfather Auantavarman Vajrahasta. The other kings who describe themselves in their inscriptions as belonging to the Gāṅga dynasty are included in group II. Kings not included in these two groups, but known to have ruled in Kaliṅga during the period under review, are included in group 1.

I. Early Kalinga Kings

This group includes thc following kings :—

1. Mahārāja Caṇḍavarman, known from the Komarti Plates[1]. The grant was issued by him from Vijaya-Siṁhapura (victorious city of Siṁhapura) in the year 6, and he is described therein as Kaliṅgādhipatiḥ or Lord of Kaliṅga. The seal of the copper-plates has the legend 'pitṛ-bhaktaḥ'.

1. Ep. Ind. IV, pp. 142 ff.

Another grant of a King Caṇḍavarman, also issued from Vijaya-Siṁhapura is dated in the year 4. He is described as Lord of Kaliṅga and the seal bears the legend 'pitṛ-bhaktaḥ'. On the other hand, the script of the inscription is somewhat different from that of the Komarti plates. It is therefore probable, though not certain, that both the plates refer to the same king[1].

2. Mahārāja Umavarman, known from Brihatprostha grant.[2] It was issued by him from Siṁhapura (written as Sīhapura) in the year 30, and he is referred to as Lord of Kaliṅga.

Perhaps the same king is referred to in another copper-plate found at Tekkali.[3] This was issued by Mahārāja Umavarmaṇ from the victorious city of Vardhamāna in the ninth year. The editor of this plate has remarked that 'the alphabet, language, and phraseology of the record resemble closely' those of the Brihatprostha grant. But the king is not referred to as the Lord of Kaliṅga. The seal of the plates contains the word 'pitṛ-bhaktaḥ'.

3. Mahārāja Nanda Prabhañjanavarman, known from the Chicacole plates[4]. The grant was issued by him from the victorious city of Sārapallikā and he is described as the Lord of the whole of Kaliṅga (sakala-Kaliṅgādhipatiḥ). The seal of the plates has the legend 'pitṛ-bhaktaḥ'. The alphabet and phraseology of the inscription resemble very closely those of the Komarti Plates of Caṇḍavarman.

4. Mahārāja Śaktivarman known from the Ragolu plates[5]. The grant was issued by him from the victorious city of Piṣṭapura in the year 13, and he is described as (1) Lord of Kaliṅga, (2) ornament of the Māgadha family, and (3) Vāsiṣṭhīputra. The alphabet of the inscription resembles the above grants but the phraseology is very different. The village granted, Rakaluva, has been identified with Ragolu, near Chicacole, where the plates were discovered.

---

1. Ann. Rep. Arch. Surv. 1934-5, p 64.
2. Ep. Ind. XII, pp. 4 ff.
3. J. A. H. R. S. VI (53). No facsimile is given and I am unable to verify the statements of the editor about the character of the alphabet.
4. Ind. Ant. XIII, p. 48. I. H. Q. Vol. X, p. 782.
5. Ep. Ind. XII. pp. 1 ff.

5. Mahārāja Ananta-Śaktivarman is known from a single grant issued from Vijaya-Siṁhapura in the 28th year of his reign. He is called Lord of Kaliṅga and 'an ornament of the Māṭharakula'. He granted a village in Varāhavarttani-viṣaya. The Charter was written by Arjunadatta, a name which also occurs in the Ragolu plates. The grant has been referred to the fifth century A.D. on palæographic grounds. This king Śaktivarman may be identical with or a successor of Śaktivarman of the Ragolu plates. It has been suggested that he was the son of Anantavarman ; and also, that the family name of Śaktivarman (No. 4 above) might be really Māṭhara and not Māgadha as wrongly read by Hultzsch, and that Ananta-Śaktivarman was 'a successor of Śaktivarman with the possibility of a king named Anantavarman intervening between them'. But nothing can be definitely said on any of these points[1]

6. A dynasty of three kings is known from two sets of copper-plates,[2] *viz.* Srungavarapukota[3] and Siripuram[4] grants of Anantavarman.

Both the grants were issued by Mahārāja Anantavarman Lord of Kaliṅga, son of Mahārāja Prabhañjanavarman, and grandson of Mahārāja Guṇavarman.

The Srungavarapukota grant was issued from the victorious city of Piṣṭapura. It mentions Guṇavarman as king of Devarāṣṭra (Devarāṣṭrādhipati) and Prabhañjanavarman as belonging to Vāsiṣṭha-kula. The village granted, *viz.* Kiṇḍeppa, was situated in the Tellavalli district (viṣaya).

The Siripuram grant was issued from the victorious city of Devapura, and there is a reference to Vāsiṣṭha family. The inscription seems to contain a date, but the passage is far from very clear. It reads as follows :—"*Brāhmaṇebhyaḥ aṣṭāśśaka saṁkhyabhyaḥ mahāśvayuje Samvatsare.* Mr. M. Narasimham, who edited the plate in the Telugu Journal Bhāratī, takes the passage to

1. Ann. Rep. Arch. Surv. 1934-5, p. 65.
2. J. A H. R. S. VIII. pp. 153 ff.
3. Ep. Ind. Vol. XXIII. p. 56.
4. This grant was published in the Telugu Journal Bhārati of September 1931, which I have not been able to utilise. Through the kindness of the Government Epigraphist I obtained an excellent estampage from which I have read the original inscription.

mean that the grant was made in the Śaka year 8 (=86 A.D.). This is, of course, absurd. The expression *'āṣṭāśśaka saṁkhyabhyaḥ* may qualify the word *'brāhmaṇebhyaḥ'*. It may also denote a date, but then the meaning is not clear.

7. Another king who ruled in Kaliṅga during the period is Viśākhavarman, known from Koroshanda copper-plates[1]. The grant was issued from the victorious city of Śrīpura in the seventh regnal year of the king, and is dated in the year 183. By this grant the king granted the village Tampoyaka in Korāsoḍaka-Pacālī to a few Brāhmaṇas.

The king does not assume the title 'lord of Kaliṅga'. But as the editor of the plate suggests, there is little doubt that Korāsoḍaka-Pacālī is the same as the division Korāsodaka-Pañcālī, referred to in the Chicacole grant of the Gāṅga king Indravarman, and comprised the region round the modern village Koroṣhaṇḍa, where the plates were found. The capital city of the king, Śrīpura, has also been identified by the editor with modern Siripuram (18°-53′ N.×83°-50′ E) in the Vizagapatam district.

If we now proceed to analyse the above records, the first thing that strikes us is the continued existence of Devarāṣṭra and Piṣṭapura, the two kingdoms in Kaliṅga which are referred to in the Allahabad Pillar inscription. Guṇavarman is expressly referred to as the king of Devarāṣṭra, while Śaktivarman was a king of Piṣṭapura. Anantavarman, the grandson of Guṇavarman, issued one of his records from Piṣṭapura, and this shows that under him the two kingdoms were united. Of course, it is quite likely that both formed one kingdom even under Śaktivarman and Guṇavarman, but of this we have no evidence. It is interesting to note in this connection that the Cālukya records refer to both Piṣṭapura and Devarāṣṭra[2].

King Anantavarman issued one of his records from Devapura, and no mention is made herein about his grandfather being lord

1. Ep. Ind., Vol. XXI, pp. 23 ff.

2. Piṣṭapuram was conquered by Pulakesi II (Aihole Ins. V. 27 ; Ep. Ind. VI, p. 6). Devarāṣṭra is referred to in the Kasimkota plates of the E. Cālukya king Bhīma I. along with Elamañci Kaliṅgadeśa (S. Ind. Ep. Rep. 1908-9., p. 109). According to G. J. Dubreuil, Elamañci formed part of the province of Devarāṣṭra. (Anc. Hist. Deccan, p. 60).

of Devarāṣṭra. But the other record issued from Piṣṭapura expressly mentions this fact. It would not be unreasonable to assume, therefore, that up to the time of the first record Anantavarman was the ruler of Devarāṣṭra with Devapura as its capital. Later he became the ruler of Piṣṭapura also, and transferred his capital there. Hence in the records of this period mention is made of the fact that his grandfather was ruler of Devarāṣṭra, a fact too obvious to be stated in the earlier records.

It is interesting to note that Śaktivarman of Piṣṭapura is called Vāsiṣṭhīputra, while Anantavarman is said to belong to the Vāsiṣṭha family. The two may, therefore, belong to the same family.

King Śaktivarman is said to be an ornament of the Māgadha family. This may be taken to imply that his family originally came from Magadha. But Māgadha is also the name of a well-known caste or clan in ancient Indian literature, and it is difficult to arrive at any definite conclusion in the matter. Besides, as already noted above, Māgadha may be a misreading for Māṭhara.

Another kingdom in Kaliṅga lay further north, with Siṁhapura as its capital. This place has been identified with modern Singapuram, a village near Chicacole. Kings Caṇḍavarman, Umavarman, and Ananta-Śaktivarman issued their records from this city.

Siṁhapura was the capital of a Kaliṅga kingdom even as late as the twelfth century A.D.[1] The foundation of a city called Siṁhapura, by Siṁhabāhu, is told in Mahāvaṁsa. As Siṁhabāhu's mother was the daughter of a princess of Kaliṅga, this city of Siṁhapura may be an echo of the Kaliṅga capital, but the whole story is too legendary to be considered seriously.

Whether the two kings Caṇḍavarman and Umavarman who ruled in Siṁhapura belonged to the same family cannot be exactly ascertained. The word 'pitṛbhaktaḥ' on the seal of king Umavarman of the Tekkali plates connects him with king Caṇḍavarman, the seal of whose copper-plates bears the same legend, but it is not possible to form any sure conclusion.

If we identify the two kings named Umavarman, the most reasonable inference seems to be that uptil the ninth year of his

1. This point will be discussed later more fully.

reign he did not obtain sovereignty over Kaliṅga. Till then he probably ruled over a kingdom with Vardhamāna as its centre. Sometime later in life he conquered Kaliṅga and assumed the title Lord of Kaliṅga. Probably at the same time he changed his seat of government to Siṁhapura.

The city of Vardhamāna naturally reminds us of the city of that name in Western Bengal. But until further evidence is available it would be risky to assume that a king of this locality obtained the sovereignty of Kaliṅga.

A fourth kingdom, with Śrīpura as capital, is known from the grant of Viśākhavarman.

Only one king now remains to be dealt with, *viz.* Nanda Prabhañjanavarman (No. 3). It has been suggested that the king's name was really Prabhañjanavarman, while the prefix Nanda is added to indicate that he belonged to the Nanda family.[1] If it were so, it would be tempting to identify him with the father of Anantavarman. But apart from the similarity of the name, there is no other evidence in support of this. On the other hand, the alphabet and phraseology of his records, as well as the seal of the legend, rather connect him with the kings of Siṁhapura, though it is difficult to agree with Mr. D.C. Sircar "that Caṇḍavarman and Nanda Prabhañjanavarman must have belonged to the same dynasty."[2]

The grant of Nanda Prabhañjanavarman was issued from Sārapallikā, which was probably his capital, though Mr. Sircar thinks that the use of the term 'Vāsaka' after the city probably suggests that it was not so.[3] No definite location of this place is possible, but it may be pointed out that there is a village called Sareapully, twelve miles north-east of Parlakimedi. Local investigations might throw some light on its probable identification with Sārapallikā.

The fact that all the kings mentioned above except Viśākhavarman bore the title 'Lord of Kaliṅga' may be taken to indicate that they all ruled over the entire region known by that name, *i.e.* from the Mahānadī to the Godāvarī. Prof. Jouveau-Dubreuil remarks :

1. Sircar-Sātavāhanas, p. 66 fn. 2.
2. I. H. Q., Vol. X, p. 782.
3. Ibid.

"In fact, the capital of the kings of Kaliṅga which was Pishṭāpuram (*sic*) at the times of Mahendra and Vāsiṣṭhīputra Śaktivarman seems to have been transferred further north to Sarapalli and Siṁhapura after the Viṣṇukuṇḍins captured Pishṭāpuram".[1]

Now there is nothing to show that Mahendra was ever a king of Kaliṅga as a whole. The Allahabad Pillar inscription simply mentions him as king of Piṣṭapura, and, as we have seen above, there was even at that time at least one other kingdom in Kaliṅga, *viz.* Devarāṣṭra. No question of the kingdom of Kaliṅga arises in the time of Samudragupta, as his inscription never refers to this term. The probability is that in his time the whole region, known as Kaliṅga, was divided into a number of small independent states. Mr. R. Subba Rao,[2] while acknowledging this, still maintains that "in Samudragupta's time, the capital of Kaliṅga was Mahendragiri-Kothur". This geographical name is a curious compound, and there is no justification for the view of Mr. Rao.

The use of the term Lord of Kaliṅga may, therefore, be taken to signify a change in the political condition, and the establishment of a united kingdom of Kaliṅga. At the same time it is well to remember how such terms are often used in a very loose manner in official records. The use of the adjective '*sakala*' (whole) before Kaliṅga in the inscription of Nanda Prabhañjanavarman may be taken to imply that Kaliṅga by itslef did not necessarily mean the whole of that region.

We are not, therefore, justified, in the absence of further evidence, to take every one of the kings mentioned above as ruler of the whole of Kaliṅga, though this is a possibility which we must by no means ignore. But the regular use of the term 'Lord of Kaliṅga' may be certainly taken to imply that the sovereignty over a united kingdom of Kaliṅga was the political ideal of the period, which was at least occasionally realised in practice. The rude invasion of Samudragupta probably facilitated the unity of Kaliṅga, in very much the same way as the invasion of Alexander did in the case of Northern India.

As evidence in support of this we may cite, in addition to the epithet 'the lord of the whole of Kaliṅga' assumed by Nanda

1. Anc. Hist. Deccan, p. 94.
2. J. A. H. R. S. VI. p. 61.

Prabhañjanavarmadeva, the fact that Śaktivarman, the ruler of Piṣṭapura, must have exercised sovereignty almost as far north as Siṁhapura, as he granted a village near Chicacole.

Finally we come to the question of the date of these kings. In this respect palaeography is at present our sole guide. We may accept as our standard the Peddavegi plates of the Śālaṅkāyaṇa king Vijayanandivarman or Nandivarman II, the great-grandson of Hastivarman. There is hardly any doubt that the latter is identical with Hastivarman, king of Veṅgi, mentioned in the Allahabad Pillar inscription. Now Hultzsch, while editing the Komarti plates of Caṇḍavarman remarked as follows :[1]

"In two other respects a connection may be established with the plates of the Śālaṅkāyaṇa *Mahārāja* Vijayanandivarman, who, like Chaṇḍavarman, professes to have been 'devoted to the feet of the lord, (his) father,' and who was the eldest son of the *Mahārāja* Chaṇḍavarman. The close resemblance between the alphabets of the plates of Vijayanandivarman and of the Komarti plates suggests that Chaṇḍavarman, the father of Vijayanandivarman, may have been identical with the *Mahārāja* Chaṇḍavarman who issued the Komarti plates. At any rate, the two Chaṇḍavarmans must have belonged to the same period."

Mr. D. C. Sircar[2] has shown some strong reasons against the identification proposed by Dr. Hultzsch. But there is hardly any doubt that the two kings belong approximately to the same period. Chaṇḍavarman of the Komarti plates may therefore be referred to the end of the fourth or the beginning of the fifth century A.D.

So far as it is possible to judge from palaeography, making due allowances for local characteristics or peculiarities of the scribe, it would be reasonable to assign all the records discussed above within a century, or, at the utmost, two centuries of the Komarti plates. We would, therefore, be quite safe if we place the early kings of Kaliṅga, mentioned above, during the period between 350 and 550 A.D., though in my opinion there is a great probability that all or most of them flourished during the fifth century A.D. Beyond

1. Ep. Ind. IV, p. 143.

2. Sātavāhanas, pp. 64-5.

this rough estimate it is not possible to determine the dates of these kings more precisely until fresh evidence is forthcoming.

Only a single inscription, that of Viśākhavarman, bears a definite date, *viz.* year 183. The editor of the Plates has observed that its alphabet 'resembles that of the Peddavegi plates of the Śālaṅkāyana king Nandivarman II and of the Brihatprostha grant of Umavarman.' We may, therefore, refer the year 183 to the Gupta era, and the accession of Viśākhavarman would then fall in the year 496 A.D. The use of the Gupta era in 503 A.D. probably indicates, and is due to the fact, that the Gāṅga era had not yet been established.

II. Early Ganga Kings

This group consists of a large number of kings who expressly describe themselves in their records as belonging to the Gāṅga dynasty. Besides, their records show the following common characteristics.

1. They all begin with a set phrase of great length : "*amara-purānukāriṇaḥ sarvartusukha*" *etc.* with some definite modifications in course of time.[1]

2. With two exceptions, they are all issued from Kaliṅga-nagara.

3. They are all dated in the year of an era which is usually described as '*pravardhamāna-vijaya-rājya-saṁvatsara*', and occasionally with the words "*Gāṅgeya-vaṁśa*" prefixed to it.

---

1. Mr. S. Rajguru has discussed in detail the gradual modifications of the opening phrases of the Gāṅga records, and has traced three stages of development (J. A. H. R. S., Vol. IV, pp. 16-17). Although his classification, on the whole, presents a good view of the modifications gradually introduced in course of time, it cannot be said to be wholly accurate, for variations occur in a few records. Cf *e.g.* the Purle and Chicacole Pl. of Indravarman III, Vizagapatam Pl. of Devendravarman II, the Chicacole Pl. of Devendravarman III, and the Cheedivalasa Pl. of Devendravarman IV (for references, see below.). It is, therefore, difficult to accept Mr. Rajguru's statement that "we can clearly trace the approximate period of any king of this line of Gāṅga dynasty only by examining the *Birudas* stated in his grant." (op. cit., p. 17).

With the help of the numerous records of this dynasty that have so far come to light, we can draw the following list of kings with dates.

1. Indravarman. 39[1]
2. Hastivarman (Raṇabhīta, Rājasiṁha). 79, 80[2]
3. [Indravarman II[3]. 87, 91, 128, 137, 138, 154.]

Or

3. [Indravarman II. (Rājasiṁha). 87, 91
4. Dānārṇava
5. Indravarman III, son of No. 4. 128, 137, 138, 154]
6. Guṇārṇava
7. Devendravarman I, son of No. 6.[4] 183, 184, 192, 195

---

1. Jirjingi Grant, year 39 ; J. A. H. R. S. III, p. 49.
2. (i) Narasingapalli Pl, year 79 ; Ep. Ind. Vol. XXIII, p. 62.
   (ii) Urlam Pl. year 80 ; Ep. Ind. XVII, pp. 332-3.
3. It is doubtful whether all the dates belong to one and the same king who would then have a reign of at least 67 years. This is not, of course, impossible, but most probably there were two kings of that name. The grant of the year 154 refers to Indravarman as son of Dānārṇava. According to all probability the earlier Indravarman (II) ruled in 87 and 91 (in these inscriptions he is called Rājasiṁha), then came Dānārṇava, and then the latter's son Indravarman III with dates 128, 137, 138, and 154.

   The dates are obtained from the following records :

   (i) Achyutapuram Pl. year 87. Ep. Ind. III, p. 128.
   (ii) Sontabomali Pl. year 87. J. A. H. R. S. IV, p. 21.
   (iii) Parlakimidi Pl. year 91. Ind. Ant. XVI, p 134.
   (iv) Chicacole Pl. year 128. Ind. Ant. XIII, p. 121. Mr. J. C. Ghosh reads the date as 101 and assigns it to the reign of Indravarman II (J. B. O. R. S. Vol. XX, pp. 45 ff.)
   (v) Purle Pl. year 137 (formerly read as 149) ; Ep. Ind. XIV, p. 361 ; the date is corrected in Ep. Ind. XVIII, p. 308.
   (vi) Chicacole Pl. year 138. Ind. Ant. XIII, p. 123. (The date was fomerly read as 146, but subsequently corrected in Ep. Ind. XVIII, p. 308.)
   (vii) Tekkali Pl. year 154, Ep. Ind. XVIII, p. 307.
4. (i) Chicacole Pl. year 183, Ep. Ind. III, p. 131.
   (ii) Dharmaliṅgeśvara Pl. year 184, J. A. H. R. S. II, 275.
   (iii) Tekkali Pl. year 192, I. H. Q. Vol. XI, p. 300.
   (iv) Siddhantam Pl. year 195, Ep. Ind. XIII, p. 213.

8. Anantavarman I, son of No. 7.[1] 204

|

9. Devendravarman II, son of No. 8.[2] 254

10. Rājendravarman I,

|

11. Anantavarman II, son of No. 10.[3] 304

12. Devendravarman III, son of No. 10.[4] 308, 310

|

13. Anantavarman III, son of No. 12.[5] 314

|

14. Rājendravarman II, son of No. 13.[6] 342

15. Satyavarman, son of No. 12 (?)[7] 351

16. Bhūpendravarman

|

17. Devendravarman V, son of No. 16.[8] 397

---

1. Dharmaliṅgeśvara Pl. year 204; J. A. H. R. S. II, p. 273.

2. Vizagapatam Pl. year 254; Ind. Ant. XVIII, p. 143.

3. Alamanda Pl. year 304; Ep. Ind. III, p. 18. Mr. Subba Rao refers to a grant dated 284, but the authority cited by him (S. Ind. Ep. Rep. 1918, pp. 137; 1924, pp. 97-8) refers to no such grant.

4. (i) Indian Museum Plates, year 308; Ep. Ind. Vol. XXIII, pp. 73 ff.
(ii) Tekkali Pl. year 310, Ep. Ind. XVIII, p. 311.
(iii) Bangalore Pl. Ep. Carn. Vol. IX, Bangalore No. 140.
(iv) Chicacole Pl. J. A. H. R. S. VIII, p. 192. C. P. No. 7 of 1918-19.

5. (i) The Nāmpali Grant of Yuvarāja Rajendravarman, son of Ana (nta) varman, dated 314, J. O. R. R., Vol. IX, p. 59.

(ii) Chicacole Pl. of Anantavarman, son of Devendravarman; J. A. H. R. S. VIII, p. 193. The inscription contains no date, but the editor has on good grounds identified Devendravarman with king No. 13.

6. Mandasa Pl. year 342. Epigraphical Report 1918, p. 137; 1924 p. 97. Mr. Subba Rao refers to a grant dated 313 but the authority cited by him (Ep. Report, 1918, p. 137; 1924, p. 97) refers to no such grant.

7. Chicacole Plates, Ind. Ant. XIV, p. 11; Bhandarkar's List No. 1484.

8. Cheedivalasa Pl. J. A. H. R. S, II, p. 146.

The list differs in some respects from the one given by Prof. Subba Rao, the latest writer on the subject, [1] and it is necessary to say a few words on each of the points on which I have differed from him.

1. The first king in Mr. Rao's list is the donor of Trilingi plates[2]. As only the last set of these plates is preserved, the name of the king is lost. The date has been read as 'pravardhamāna-rājya-samvatsarasy-āṣṭhāvimsatāni.' But although the reading is very doubtful, this date, *viz.* year 28, has been taken by both the editor of the plates and Mr. Rao to refer to Gāṅga era. One important point has, however, been ignored by both of them. The writer of the plates, Vinayacandra, son of Bhānucandra, also engraved the plates of Hastivarman, dated 79 and 80, and those of Indravarman dated 87 and 91, while the son of Vinayacandra engraved the plates dated 128. Now if the Trilingi plates are dated in the same era, we have to suppose that Vinayacandra was actively engaged in his office for nearly sixty-five to seventy years (allowing some years before 28 and after 91), while his son was actively engaged in his office more than one hundred years after his father had entered the office. This is highly improbable, if not impossible. Besides, the writer of the Jirjingi grant dated 39 is a different person. Mr. J. C. Ghosh reads the date as 88 (eighty-eight) [3]. This is more likely, and in that case the plate would belong to the reign of Indravarman II.

2. The second name in Mr. Rao's list is Mitavarma. This is the name of the father of Indrādhirāja of the Eastern region, referred to in the Godāvarī plates of Pṛthivīmūla (see below). Mr. Rao identifies this Indrādhirāja with Indravarman (No. 1 in my list) and hence regards Mitavarma as his father. But the identification is very problematical, and hence it will be unwise to take Mitavarman as the father of Indravarman I. For all we know, he might have been father of Indravarman II.

---

1. Mr. Rao dealt with the subject in a series of articles in J. A. H. R. S. V (193, 261); VI (57, 69, 193); VII (57, 125, 181, 231); VIII (41). The list of the Early Gāṅga kings is given in J. A. H. R. S. Vol. V, pp. 275-6.

2. The Tirlingi Plates were edited in J. A. H. R. S. III, p. 54. For Mr. Rao's views cf. J. A. H. R. S, VI, pp. 69-70.

3. J. B. O. R. S. Vol. XX, pp. 44-5.

3. Immediately after Indravarman I, Mr. Rao places three kings, Anantavarman, his son Devendravarman, and his son Satyavarman, with a date 51 for each of the last two. He relies on the two Chicacole plates of these two kings noticed by Fleet[1]. But after referring to the grant of Devendravarman dated 254, Fleet remarked as follows :

"These three grants of Devendravarma and Satyavarma are shown, by the characters in which they are engraved, to be of later date than the three grants of Indravarma [dated 91, 128 and 146 (really 138)]. Consequently the fifty-first year which is quoted in one of the grants of Devendravarma and in the grant of his son Satyavarma, cannot be referred to the same epoch with the dates of 91, 128 and 146, of Indravarma."

The criticism of Fleet seems to me eminently reasonable. He takes the date 51 of Devendravarman as equivalent to 251, and in that case he would be identical with the King No. 9. The date of Satyavarman's plate is now read as 'Gāṅgeyavaṁśa Saṁvacchara-sāta-tray-aikapañcāśat,' and this would be equivalent to 351. I have accordingly placed this king as no 15 in the list.

I may add that except in these two cases the words 'Gāṅgeya-Vaṁśa' has never been prefixed to the expression of date before the year 304 of the Gāṅga era, and this is also an additional argument in favour of a late date for these two records.

4. Mr. Rao takes Hastivarman and Indravarman II to be brothers, because both of them had the same titles 'Rājasiṁha', 'Gaṅg-āmala-kula-pratiṣṭhaḥ' and 'sakala-Kaliṅgādhirājaḥ.' The last two titles are fairly common. The common titles might as well indicate that they were father and son. No definite conclusion is, therefore, possible on this point.

5. Mr. Rao has added the name of Jayavarman after Devendravarman I, as elder brother of Anantavarman, and given them separate numbers 12 and 13. Anantavarman's inscription refers to a grant by his brother Śrī Jayavarman, but there is nothing to indicate that the latter was a king.

---

1. Ind. Ant. XIII, pp. 273 ff.

6. Mr. Rao has added after Anantavarman I the name of his son Nandavarman with a date 221, on the strength of the Santha-Bombali grant[1]. The grant was issued by Mahārāja Śrī-mānaṁda-varmmā, son of Śrī Anantavarmmā. The name has been emended as Srīmān-Nanda Varmmā. This is not inadmissible, but the real difficulty is about the date. The editor has read the date as 'samvacchara śate 221.' But the letter after the word 'samvacchara' is certainly not *śa* but looks like a numerical symbol for 50. The portion which the editor reads as 221 is illegible on the published plate. There has been some controversy regarding the accuracy of the date[2]. Until clearer estampage of the portion containing the date is available it is not possible to make a final decision.

7. The genealogy from Devendravarman II to Rājendravarman II is somewhat different in my list.

In his genealogical list, Mr. Rao makes Rājendravarman (No 10) a son of Devendravarman II (No 9),[3] but I do not know of any authority for the same. While discussing Rājendravarman's son Anantavarman in the body of his article he remarks: "The king's C. P. Grant dated 284, has simply been noticed in S. I. Ep. Reports [1918, pp. 137-8 ; 1924, pp. 97-8]. The details are not forthcoming but the genealogy of the kings from Guṇārṇava, the father of Devendra II, to Rājendravarma II is settled."

As regards the last named king also he cites the same authority for the statement: "Two C. P. grants of this king are merely noticed in Ep. Reports" ; and then adds : "A. C. P. grant of this king dated in G. E. 342 is also edited [J. B. O. R.S. Vol. XII, p. 101[4]"].

These statements are inaccurate and misleading. The two Epigraphic Reports cited by Mr. Rao do not contain any reference to a grant of Anantavarman dated 284, or to any new grant of Rājendravarman, other than that of 342 G. E. This is not edited in J.B.O.R.S., as Mr. Rao suggests. In his genealogical list Mr. Rao

1. J. A. H. R. S. II, p. 185.
2. J. A. H. R. S. III, p. 75, IV, p. 9.
3. J. A. H. R. S. Vol. V, p. 276.
4. J. A. H. R. S. Vol. VI, pp. 196-7.

refers to a grant of Rājendravarman of the year 313 and cites the same two Epigraphic Reports as his authority, but they contain no reference to any such grant.

As regards the genealogy from Guṇārṇava to Rājendravarman II being settled, presumably he refers to the genealogical tree given in the two Epigraphic Reports. But neither he nor the author of these Reports has taken into consideration king Anantavarman III, No. 13 in my list. This king is referred to as the son of Devendravarman, and as regards the last, obviously the choice lies between No. 9 and No. 12 of my list. But the palæography and the phraseology of Anantavarman's grant resemble those of the latter and differ from those of the former. Hence his father should be identified rather with No. 12 than with No. 9. Once this is conceded, it appears more reasonable that Anantavarman, father of Rājendravarman II (No. 15 in my list), should be identified with the king No. 13 rather than with No. 11. Thus the genealogy would be as follows :—

No. 10 Rājendravarman I

11. Anantavarman II (304) | 12. Devendravarman III (308, 310)

15. Satyavarman (351) | 13. Anantavarman III

14. Rājendravarman II (342)

8. Before Bhūpendravarman (No. 16) Mr. Rao places two kings Mārasiṁha, his father, and Vajri or Vajrahasta, his grandfather. He relies on the following verse in the Cheedivalasa plates of Devendravarman.

"*Mārasiṁha pitā yasya Vajri caiva pitāmahaḥ* ।

Svayam Devendravarmeti sutis sadguṇakīrtanam ॥

He has proposed the amendment 'sūti' instead of 'suti.' The first letter is very doubtful, though in the published facsimile it looks more like 'stuti' than anything else. But the fact remains that the pronoun 'yasya' can only refer to Devendravarmā himself, as the preceding passage only refers to him (cf. *e.g.* the passage *Yasmin vasumatīṁ pāti, etc.* which immediately precedes the verse).

The word '*svayam*' that precedes 'Devendravarmā' also shows that he is the person referred to in the passage cited. The word '*iti*' concludes the long phrase which stands in apposition to the two words that follow. As such the terms *pitā* and *pitāmaha* can only refer to the father and grandfather of Devendravarman himself, and not to those of his father as Mr. Rao interprets.

It would, therefore, follow that Mārasiṁha was an epithet of Devendravarman's father Bhūpendravarman, and similarly we should take 'Vajri' as the epithet, rather than the proper name of his grandfather.

Having thus settled the list of kings, we may now proceed to discuss their history.

The sequence of the kings is settled by the dates in their records and there is no difficulty caused by overlapping. This, coupled with the facts that all of them belonged to the Gāṅga family and all (except No. 1) issued their grants from Kaliṅganagara[1], leads to the conclusion that the kings all belonged to the same dynasty which exercised sway over Kaliṅga without any break for nearly four hundred years.

The period during which the kings ruled in Kaliṅga can be accurately determined only by fixing the initial point of the era which was used in their records ; for although most of the inscriptions do not expressly refer to the Gāṅga era, it is unanimously held by the scholars that all the dates are to be referred to an era established by the Gāṅgas, and which is called either in full 'Gāṅgavaṁśa-pravardhamāna-vijayarājya-samvatsara' or simply as 'pravardhamāna-vijayarājya-samvatsara.'

Various theories are current about the epoch of the era, and I have discussed the question in a separate article.[2] I have tried to show that so far at least as the present available data go, the most reasonable conclusion seems to be that the era was started within a few years of 550 A.D. and most probably between 550 and 557 A.D. Without claiming for this hypothesis any

1. The Purle Plates of Indravarman III, like the Jirjiṅga grant of Indravarman I, are issued from Dantapura. But the other plates of Indravarman III are issued from Kaliṅganagara.

2. Indian Culture, Vol. IV, p. 171.

finality or decisive character, I shall proceed to discuss the history of the Gāṅgas on this basis.

It would appear that this dynasty first came into political prominence about the middle of the sixth century A.D. It was a period of great upheaval in the political atmosphere of India. The Gupta empire finally collapsed before the onslaught of Yaśodharman who carried his conquests as far as Mahendra mountain, in the very heart of Kaliṅga.[1] The deity named Gokarṇa-svāmī on the summit of this hill was an object of special veneration to the Gāṅgas and is always referred to in the introductory portion of their records. It seems likely, therefore, that the Gāṅgas came into prominence after this region was freed from the control of Yaśodharman.

The Maukharī king Īśānavarman followed in the wake of Yaśodharman, and claims victories in Andhradeśa and Kośala.[2] Although there is no reference to Kaliṅga, it is possible that this intermediate region was also affected.

But far more important for Kaliṅga was the rise of the Cālukyas in the Central Deccan and the growing power of the Viṣṇukuṇḍins in Veṅgi, about the middle of the sixth century A.D.

When old political systems were crumbling into dust and new ones were taking their places, the time was opportune for a new dynasty to come into prominence. The Gāṅgas played their part well, and established their sway over a large part of Kaliṅga after the northern invasions had spent up their force. Perhaps they built on the ruins in which Kaliṅga was overwhelmed by the calamities of foreign conquests.

But the Gāṅgas were not masters of the whole of Kaliṅga. The northern part of it, comprising the territories round the Chilka Lake and the modern districts of Cuttack and Puri formed a separate kingdom under the name Koṅgoda, and was ruled by the Śailodbhava dynasty, almost throughout the period that the Gāṅgas were ruling in Kaliṅga. The history of this dynasty has been dealt with in a separate article[3].

1. Mandasor Ins. Fleet—Gupta Ins. p. 146.
2. Haraha Ins. Ep. Ind. Vol. XIV. p. 110.
3. J. A. H. R. S. Vol. X, pp. 1-15.

As to the western boundary, king Indravarman I is called Tri-Kaliṅgādhipati, or Lord of Tri-Kaliṅga. Tri-Kaliṅga has been usually interpreted as denoting the whole of Kaliṅga in its widest extent. The title was also assumed by the Eastern Gāṅga king Vajrahasta III (or V, according to another reckoning). Prof. Subba Rao, while adhering to the usual interpretation of Tri-Kaliṅga, gives different connotations to it in these two cases. In the case of Vajrahasta he says : "He was also the paramount sovereign of Tri-Kaliṅga country which extended from the river Ganges in the North to the river Godavari in the South."[1] But, referring to the title 'Tri-Kaliṅgādhipati' of Indravarman I, he remarks : "This title would suggest that he ruled over the whole country extending from the Chilka Lake in the north to the river Godavari in the South."[2]

Prof. Subba Rao does not make it clear why he puts these two different interpretations on the same term. But the explanation is obvious. The occupation of Koṅgoda by the Śailodbhavas makes it unlikely that Indravarman I could ever extend his suzerainty beyond the Chilka Lake, and hence Prof. Rao was constrained to take Tri-Kaliṅga in this case in a restricted sense. But this very fact should give us a warning against the acceptance of the usual meaning of the term. As a matter of fact, the references to Kaliṅga and Tri-Kaliṅga in the records of the Eastern Cālukya kings, which are quoted a few pages later, would leave no doubt that Tri-Kaliṅga meant a region, distinct from, and much less important than, Kaliṅga, and was presumably a wild region covered with hills and forests. These records support the hypothesis of Mr. G. Ramdas that Tri-Kaliṅga denotes the highland to the west of the Mahendra hills of Ganjam from the upper course of the Mahānadi to about the source of the Lāṅguliyā river[3]. Perhaps it would be safer to take Tri-Kaliṅga as a general name for the hilly tracts, lying to the west of Kaliṅga, and separating it from the Central Provinces. This region evidently shared the fate of all borderlands and passed at different times into the hands of the Haihayas,

1. J. A. H. R. S., Vol. VI, p. 203.
2. Ibid, p. 73.
3. J. B. O. R. S., Vol. XIV., pp. 539 ff. ; Vol. XV, pp. 635 ff.

Candellas, and the Somavaṁśi kings of Kośala on the one side, and the Gāṅgas and the Cālukyas on the other. The records of all these dynasties refer to some of their kings as Lord of Tri-Kaliṅga. While this fact can be easily reconciled with the identification of Tri-Kaliṅga proposed above, it would be ridiculous, if, on the basis of the usually accepted meaning of Tri-Kaliṅga, we hold that those rulers established even nominal suzerainty over the whole of Kaliṅga *i.e.*, the region extending from the Ganges (or even from the Chilka Lake) to the Godāvarī.

By accepting the proposed identification we may regard Indravarman I as ruling over the hilly tracts to the west of Kaliṅga. As the title 'Lord of Tri-Kaliṅga' was not assumed by any other king it may be presumed that the region was soon lost to the family[1].

Let us now turn to the southern part of Kaliṅga. Here the Gāṅgas first came into conflict with the Viṣṇukuṇḍins. The Pulomburu plates of king Mādhavavarman[2] inform us that while the king had crossed the Godāvarī with a view to the conquest of the eastern region, he granted the village of Pulomburu to a Brāhmaṇa named Śivaśarmā. This village is no doubt the same as modern Polamuru, where the inscription was discovered, near the Anaparti Railway station in the East Godāvarī district. Thus it appears that Mādhavavarman led an expedition against Kaliṅga and conquered at least a portion of its southern territories. Again the Viṣṇukuṇḍin king Indravarman or Indrabhaṭṭāraka granted a village in the Plaki-rāṣṭra, which corresponds to the modern Vizagapatam district[3]. This shows a still further advance into Kaliṅga.

---

1. According to Hiuen Tsang 'Kaliṅga was 5000 li in circuit but it was sparsely populated.' He further remarks that "the forests and jungle are continuous for many hundred li" (Beal's Transl., Vol. II pp. 207-8). From this it may be gathered that Tri-Kaliṅga formed a part of Kaliṅga when the pilgrim visited it about 639 A. D.

2. J. A. H. R. S., Vol. VI. p. 17. D. C. Sircar—'The successors of the Śatavāhanas in the Eastern Deccan.' Journ. Dep. Letters, Cal. Univ. Vol. XXVI, p. 93.

3. Ramatirtham Pl. Ep. Ind. XII, 133. For the identification of Plaki-rāṣṭra, cf. J-Dubreuil—Anc. Hist. Deccan, p. 91.

The struggle between the Viṣṇukuṇḍin king Indrabhaṭṭāraka and a confederacy of kings headed by Indrādhirāja of the East is referred to in the Godāvarī plates of Pṛthivīmūla[1]. This Indrādhirāja, as noted by Fleet, was almost certainly a king of Kaliṅga. For 'the figurative expression that the Adhirāja Indra mounted upon the elephant Supratika of the north-east quarter, overthrew the elephant Kumuda of the south-east or southern quarter shows that the kingdom of Adhirāja Indra was to the north-east of Veṅgī'. Fleet very naturally therefore suggested the identification of Adhirāja Indra with the only Gāṅga king of that name then known, *viz*. Indravarman, with dates 128 and 146 (*i.e.* Indravarman III). Later, while editing the Parlakimidi plates of Indravarman II he thought it possible that Adhirāja Indra might be identified with this Gāṅga king. Since then we have come to know of another Gāṅga king of this name, *viz*. Indravarman I, and Mr. Subba Rao has identified him with Adhirāja Indra.

Unfortunately we have to deal here with two unknown quantities. The chronology and even the order of succession of the Viṣṇukuṇḍin kings is far from being settled yet, and although we know the dates, in Gāṅga era, of all the three Gāṅga kings bearing the name Indravarman, we are unable to assign any positive dates to them so long as the epoch of the Gāṅga era is not finally determined.

Proceeding on the basis that the Gāṅga era was started between 550 and 557 A.D., I would identify Adhirāja Indra with Indravarman I with date 39 (=c. 593 A.D.). As to Indrabhaṭṭāraka, Mr. Subba Rao[2] refers him to about 500 A.D. and places him about three generations before king Mādhavavarman who issued the Pulomburu plates. Mr. D. C. Sircar on the other hand places Indrabhaṭṭāraka three generations after the latter, and assigns to him the date 625 to 655 A.D.[3].

---

1. J. Bo. Br. R. A. S. XVI, p. 116. Fleet, who edited this inscription, identified king Indrabhaṭṭāraka with the Eastern Cālukya king of that name, the younger brother of Jayasiṁha I. J. Dubreuil's view that he is to be identified with the Viṣṇukuṇḍin king is now generally accepted (Sircar-Sātavāhanas, p. 98.)

2. J. A. H. R. S. VI, p. 19.

3. Sātavāhanas, p. 97.

Without expressing any opinion on these dates, I may point out that the struggle between the Viṣṇukuṇḍins and the Gāṅgas must almost certainly be placed before the Cālukya king Pulakeśin II inflicted a disastrous defeat on both. Pulakeśin's conquest of Piṣṭapura and Veṅgī, referred to in the Aihole inscription, took place, according to Fleet, about A.D. 616[1]. According to certain interpretation of the Kopparam plates[2], the date may even be somewhat earlier. Mr. D. C. Sircar has argued against the generally accepted view that Pulakeśin conquered the whole of the kingdom of the Viṣṇukuṇḍins[3]. But even assuming the correctness of his view that the Viṣṇukuṇḍins maintained for some time a precarious existence in the small district round their capital city, it stands to reason that after Pulakeśin was master of southern Kaliṅga (at least the region round Piṣṭapura) and a large part of Veṅgī, we cannot think of the Viṣṇukuṇḍin king Indrabhaṭṭāraka advancing as far as Vizagapatam district, or of a confederacy of kings headed by a Gāṅga king of Kaliṅga, styled as Adhirāja Indra, fighting against him. With the Cālukya kingdom established in the Eastern Godāvarī district, there could not be any struggle between the Gāṅgas of Kaliṅga and the Viṣṇukuṇḍins of Veṅgī.

The fight between these two powers must therefore be referred to the latter part of the sixth century A.D. at the latest, and Indravarman I who flourished about this time may be identified with Adhirāja Indra. The result of the struggle was evidently indecisive. While Mādhavavarman and Indrabhaṭṭāraka both penetrated into the southern Kaliṅga, as noted before, the Godāvarī

1. Ind. Ant., XX. p. 94.

2. According to Lakshmana Rao the date of these plates is A. D. 611 (Ann. Bhand. Ins. IV. 43), while according to Hultzsch (Ep. Ind. XVIII, p. 257) it is 629-30 A. D. These plates record the grant of some lands in Karmarāṣṭra (northern part of Nellore and southern part of Guntur) by one Pṛthividuvarāja in the presence of Pulakeśin II. On the basis of this V. A. Smith held that Pulakeśin II "made himself master of Vengī, between the Krishnā and Godāvarī, and established his brother Kubja Vishṇuvardhana there as viceroy in A. D. 611 with his capital at the stronghold of Pishtapura, now Pithāpuram in the Godāvarī district" (Early History of India, 4th Ed. p. 441)

3. D. C. Sircar, op. cit., pp. 103-4.

plates of Pṛthivīmūla, as noted above, definitely claim the victory for Adhirāja Indra. It is likely that after the initial successes of the Viṣṇukuṇḍins, the Gāṅga king organised a confederacy against them and succeeded in driving them out of Kaliṅga.

The Tāṇḍivāḍa plates[1] refer to a king named Pṛthivi Mahārāja, son of Vikramendra and grandson of Mahārāja Raṇadurjaya, as having made a grant from Piṣṭapura in his 46th regnal year. Mr. N. Venkataramanayya, who has edited these plates refers the inscription to about 630 A. D. He thinks that Raṇadurjaya successfully rebelled against his suzerain the Viṣṇukuṇḍin king, and thus the latter lost the territory to the north of the Godāvarī, and that it was with the object of recovering this territory that Viṣṇukuṇḍin Mādhavavarman III crossed the Godāvarī in the 48th year of his reign. This, however, appears to be very unlikely, in view of the political condition of the region in 630 A.D. as noted above.

But the Viṣṇukuṇḍins were not the only enemies of the Gāṅgas. They had to fight with their northern neighbours, the Śailodbhavas of Koṅgoda, and the mighty Cālukyas of the Deccan. The Śailodbhava king Sainyabhīta II (c. 615-30 A.D.) appears to have defeated the Gāṅga king and wrested some of his territories, but the success was shortlived and the successors of Sainyabhīta do not appear to have had anything to do with Kaliṅga. The title Raṇabhīta, assumed by the Gāṅga king Hastivarman (No. 2) who flourished about this time, may be ascribed to his intimate association with the Śailodbhava dynasty whose kings had titles ending in 'bhīta.'

But the Cālukyas proved to be a more dangerous enemy of the Gāṅgas than either the Viṣṇukuṇḍins or the Śailodbhavas.

As already noted above, the Cālukya king Pulakeśin defeated the Kośalas and Kaliṅgas in or about 616 A.D., and permanently annexed the region round Piṣṭapura which henceforth formed a part of the Eastern Cālukya kingdom.[2] The copper-plate grants

1. Tāṇḍivāda Plates of Pṛthivī Mahārāja (J.Or.R., Vol. IX, pp. 188 ff).

2. The conquests of Pulakeśin are described in the Aihole Ins. (Ep. Ind. VI, p. 1.) The defeat of the Kaliṅgas is referred to in v. 26, and the conquest of Piṣṭapura in v. 27. Cf. the statement of V. A. Smith quoted on p. 22 fn. 2.

of the Eastern Cālukyas show that they extended their suzerainty to modern Vizagapatam, or at least to its southern part. Occasionally they claimed to have exacted tributes from Kaliṅga and even to have actually ruled over Kalinga and Tri-Kaliṅga. In support of these propositions, and in order to define more clearly the status of the Gāṅga kings and the extent of their kingdom in Kaliṅga, a few facts culled from the inscriptions of the Eastern Cālukyas are noted below :

1. The E. Cālukya king Viṣṇuvardhana, from his residence at Cerupura, in Plaki-Viṣaya, grants a village in the Dimila-Viṣaya. Cerupura has been identified with Chipurupalli, and Dimila with the modern village of Dimile, both in the Vizagapatam district.[1] The date of this grant is 633 A.D.

2. The same king, from his residence at Piṣṭapura, granted lands in the Palaki Viṣaya, *i.e.* the Plaki-Viṣaya of the above grant.[2]

3. Jayasiṁha I. (633-663 A.D.) grants the village of Pulimburu, modern Polamuru, near Anaparti Railway Station in E. Godāvarī district.[3]

4. Indrabhaṭṭāraka (663 A.D.) grants a village, bounded on the south by Cerupūru (*i.e.* Chipurupalli, see. no. 1).[4]

5. Kokilivarma Mahārāja, the grandson of the E. Cālukya king Maṅgivarman (usually referred to as Maṅgi-yuvarāja, and reigning from A. D. 672 to 696), and the son of Vinayādityavarman, granted, from his residence (Vāsaka) at Elamañci (modern Yellamanchili), villages situated in Bhogipura-Viṣaya to Brāhmaṇas resident in Muñjeṛu. The Bhogipura-Viṣaya, described as situated in Madhyama-Kaliṅga, was "evidently named after the modern Bhogāpuram in the Bimlipatam -tāluka of the Vizagapatam district". Muñjeṛu is of course the modern village of the same name where the plates were discovered. It is near Bhogāpuram.[5]

1. The Chipurupalli C. P. Grant of Viṣṇuvardhana, Ind. Ant, XX, p. 15.

2. Timmapuram Pl. Ep. Ind., IX. p. 317.

3. J. A. H. R. S. IV, pp. 72-73 ; Ep. Ind. XIX, p. 254. The village is wrongly identified in the latter.

4. Ep. Ind. XVIII, p. 1.

5. Muñjeṛu copper-plates, S. Ind. Ep. Rep., 1908-9, pp. 105-6.

6. Kokkili-Vikramāditya-Bhaṭṭāraka (A. D. 709) who succeeded Jayasiṁha II (696-709 A. D.) on the throne of Veṅgī, evidently wrested Madhyama-Kaliṅga from his nephew Kokilivarma-Mahārāja, for he granted the village Muñjeṛu to the residents of Depūḍi.[1]

7. Maṅgi-Yuvarāja II, son of the king mentioned in No. 6, evidently ruled over Madhyama-Kaliṅga, even after his father had beeu deposed from the throne of Veṅgī after a rule of six months. For he granted a village in Bhogapura-Viṣaya to 103 Brāhmaṇas of Muñjeṛu.[2]

8. Some lands in the neighbourhood of Pithapuram were granted in the reign of Viṣṇuvardhana III, in the year 731 A. D.[3]

9. Vijayāditya III (844-888 A. D.) took by force the gold of the Gāṅga king of Kaliṅga [4] and received elephants as tribute from the Kaliṅga king.[5]

10. Cālukya-Bhīma I. (888-918 A. D.) grants lands in Elāmañci-Kaliṅgadesa and Devarāṣṭra.[6] The former corresponds to modern Yellamanchili.

11. Vijayāditya IV (918 A. D.) ruled the Veṅgī-maṇḍala joined with the Tri-Kaliṅga forest.[7]

12. Amma I. (918-925 A. D.), drove away his enemies from Pithapuṛam.[8]

13. Vikramāditya II (after 925 A. D.) ruled over Veṅgī and Tri-Kaliṅga.[9]

14. Amma II (945-970 A. D.) granted lands in Elamañci-Kaliṅga (see No. 7)[10]. He is described as having 'ruled well the

---

1. Ibid.
2. Ibid.
3. Ep. Ind. XVIII, p. 58. J. A. H. R. S., I., p. 89.
4. Masulipatam Pl. of Cālukya Bhīma (S. Ind. Ep. Rep. 1914, p. 84)
5. Pithapuram Ins. of Mallapadeva, Ep. Ind., Vol., IV, p. 240.
6. Kasimkoṭa Ins. (S. Ind. Ep. R. 1909, p. 108). According to G. J. Dubreuil Elamañci formed part of the province of Devarāṣṭra, Anc. Hist. Deccan, p. 60.
7. Masulipatam Pl. of Amma I. Ep. Ind. V. p. 131.
8. Pithapuram Ins. S. Ind. Ins. Vol. I, p. 42.
9. Kolavennu Grant of Cālukya-Bhīma II, S. Ind. Ins. Vol I, pp. 43 ff.
10. Pamulavaka Ins., J. A. H. R. S. Vol. II, p. 242.

Veṅgī country with Tri-Kaliṅga, according to the injunctions of Dharma' [1]. About 956 A. D. Bādapa invaded Veṅgī, and Amma II retired to Kaliṅga, leaving the throne of Veṅgī to his elder brother Dānārṇava. Amma II ruled in Kaliṅga for fourteen years more (956-970 A. D.).

15. Dānārṇava, too, had to leave Veṅgī which was captured by Bādapa, and ruled in Kaliṅga for three years (970-973 A.D.).

16. Śaktivarman, son of Dānārṇava, recovered Veṅgī in 1003 A. D.[2]

The few historical facts noted above make it evident that the provinces of Piṣṭapura and Devarāṣṭra, *i.e.*, the district of Godāvarī, and the southern part of Vizagapatam were, generally speaking, outside the dominions of the Gāṅgas almost throughout the whole course of their history. As already noted above, the northern part of Kaliṅga formed the kingdom of Koṅgoda, ruled over by the Śailodbhavas. The kingdom of the Gāṅgas therefore comprised only the territories between the two. This is further borne out by the fact that the large number of inscriptions belonging to the Gāṅgas which have hitherto come to light exclusively refer to the narrow region comprising the northern part of Vizagapatam and the southern part of Ganjam districts. It is not possible to define the boundaries more precisely, for we do not know the southern boundaries of Koṅgoda, and are unable always to locate exactly the villages referred to in the copper-plate grants of the Gāṅgas and the Eastern Cālukyas.

All the Gāṅga grants are issued from Kaliṅganagara except two which are issued from Dantapura. Kaliṅganagara was identified by Cunningham with Rājamahendri[3] and by Fleet with modern Kalingapatam[4] at the mouth of the Vaṁśadharā river, 16 miles north of Chicacole. Mr. G. V. Ramamurti proposed the identification with Mukhalingam, a village on the left bank of the Vaṁśadharā river, about 20 miles from Parlakimedi. As he points out, there are ruins of temples and other buildings all over the village and beyond

1. Ārumbāka Pl. of Bādapa. Ep. Ind. XIX. p. 137.
2. I. H. Q. Vol XI, pp. 42-5.
3. Anc. Geogr. India, p. 591.
4. Ind. Ant., XVI, p. 132.

it southwards for about two miles as far as another village, named Nagarakatakam, which belongs to the Narasannapeta *tāluka*."[1] Mr. Cunningham's identification must be given up, and the choice lies between Kalingapatam and Mukhalingam. Without going into the controversy, it will suffice to say that the known facts are undoubtedly in favour of the latter.[2]

As regards Dantapura, the city is famous in old Buddhist and Jaina literature, as the capital of Kaliṅga. Mr. G. Ramadas has suggested that "Dantapura stood on the place which is now shown as the site of the fort of Dantavaktra on the way from Chicacole to Siddhantam (Siddhārthakagrāma, a Buddhist village)."[3] M. Sylvain Lévi, starting from this basis, has sought to prove that Dantapura is identical with Ptolemy's Paloura, and is to be located on the sea-coast near Chicacole and Kalingapatam. Paloura, as he points out, was, according to Ptolemy, the *apheterium* of navigation towards the Far East *i.e*, the point where the ships, instead of keeping close to the coast, sailed direct over the seas towards the East.[4] Mr. Oldham has since definitely identified Paloura with the 'existing village of Pālūru at the northern extremity of the Ganjam district.'[5]

This identification of Dantapura removes some of the difficulties in identifying Kaliṅganagara with an inland town like Mukhaliṅgam. For there are some literary references to the capital of Kaliṅga being on the sea-coast, and these may be taken to refer to the sea-coast town of Dantapura.

The earliest copper-plate grant of the Gāṅgas is issued from Dantapura, and the only other grant of the family issued from the same place is dated about 100 years later. Dantapura may be the early seat of the family ; in any case it may be regarded as a second capital.

---

1. Ep. Ind. IV. pp. 187-8.

2. For the different views on the subject cf J. A. H. R. S., Vol. VI pp. 57 ff.

3. Ep. Ind. XIV, p. 361.

4. Lévi's article appeared in Journal Asiatique Vol. CCVI, pp. 46 ff. It has been translated into English in 'Pre-Aryan and Pre-Dravidian in India' by Dr. P. C. Bagchi, pp. 163 ff.

5. J. B. O. R. S., Vol. XXII, pp. 1 ff.

The sites of these two capitals occupy the very heart of the small kingdom over which the Gāṅgas ruled, and this fits in well with our view about its extent. Indeed, everything indicates that the Gāṅgas were a petty local dynasty ruling over a small kingdom. There is no reference in their inscriptions to any specific conquest of foreign lands, beyond mere vague general references to victories in battles which, of course, count for nothing. Hemmed in by the E. Cālukyas in the south and the Śailodbhavas in the north, they maintained their sovereignty over central Kaliṅga, which was evidently regarded as Kaliṅga proper,[1] at least during this period. It is all the more remarkable under these circumstances that they should have started an era of their own which continued in use for more than five hundred years.

Even in their narrowly circumscribed region, the Kaliṅgas had occasionally to fight with distant enemies. About the middle of the eighth century A.D., Harsha, king of Kāmarūpa overran Kaliṅga.[2] At the beginning of the ninth century A.D. the Pratīhāra king Nāgabhaṭa claims to have defeated the kings of Andhra and Kaliṅga.[3] The Andhra, no doubt, refers to the kingdom of the Eastern Cālukyas. We know that the E. Cālukya king Vijayāditya II (799-843 A. D.) conquered the Rāṣṭrakūṭa kingdom. As Dr. D. C. Ganguly has suggested, probably this king Vijayāditya also invaded the Pratīhāra dominion.[4] In that case we may suppose that the king of Kaliṅga joined the E. Cālukya king and shared his defeat. Otherwise it is difficult to account for the encounter between Nāgabhaṭa and the distant king of Kaliṅga.

---

1. We have reference to the terms, Kaliṅga, Madhyama-Kaliṅga and Tri-Kaliṅga in the records of the E. Cālukyas. There is no doubt that Madhyama-Kaliṅga roughly corresponds to Vizagapatam district, and Tri-Kaliṅga, as noted above, most probably denotes the hilly region to the west of Kaliṅga. The Gāṅga rulers systematically describe themselves as rulers of Kaliṅga, while only one of the Śailodbhava rulers refers to his suzerainty over Kaliṅga, their kingdom being always referred to as Koṅgoda in their records. Hence the presumption is natural that the kingdom of the Gāṅgas was known as Kaliṅga proper.

2. Ind. Ant.; Vol. IX. p. 178.

3. Gwaliar Praśasti of Bhoja, v. 8. Ep. Ind. Vol. XVIII, p. 112.

4. I. H. Q. Vol. IX. p. 740.

From the middle of the ninth century A. D. the E. Cālukya kings seem to have exercised supremacy over Kaliṅga. Vijayāditya III (844-888 A. D.) received tribute from the king of Kaliṅga and took gold from him by force. In the tenth century Vijayāditya IV, Vikramāditya II, and Amma II ruled over Tri-Kaliṅga. From 956 to 1003 A. D. three E. Cālukya kings ruled in Kaliṅga alone, after losing Veṅgī.

The inscription of the last Gāṅga king known so far is dated in 397 which would correspond to the middle of the tenth century A.D. We have also no record of the dynasty for nearly half a century before that. It would not, therefore, be unreasonable to presume that the end of the political supremacy of the dynasty was brought about by the E. Cālukyas. It is, of course, quite posssible that the E. Cālukyas occupied only a portion of Kaliṅga proper and the Gāṅgas ruled over the rest. But the reference to their rule over Kaliṅga and Tri-Kaliṅga naturally lead to the inference that the E. Cālukyas considerably extended their power in Kaliṅga at the expense of the Gāṅgas. The Gāṅga kings must have lost their political importance in the latter half of the ninth century A.D., and the rule of the family was brought to an end in the tenth century. This fits in well with the epigraphic data of both the Gāṅgas and the Eastern Cālukyas.